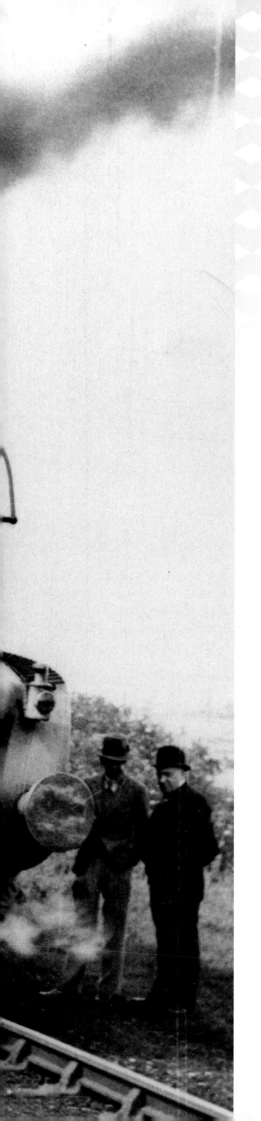

MAGNIFICENT
MALLARD
75TH ANNIVERSARY

Heritage Editor: Harri Aston
Written by: Peter Elson
Designer: Ben Renshaw

© 2013 Trinity Mirror. All Rights Reserved

Managing Director: Ken Rogers
Senior Editor: Steve Hanrahan
Senior Art Editor: Rick Cooke
Editor: Paul Dove
Senior Marketing Executive: Claire Brown
Photosales: 0845 300 3021
Images: National Railway Museum/Science & Society Picture Library, Mirrorpix, PA Photos
Printed by: William Gibbons

SPEEDING DOWN TRACK OF HISTORY

1825 – LOCOMOTION NO 1
Built for the Stockton and Darlington Railway by Robert Stephenson and Company, it was the first steam locomotive to run on a passenger-carrying line.

1829 – STEPHENSON'S ROCKET
The winner of Liverpool and Manchester Railway's Rainhill Trials, Rocket became the template for most steam engines in the following 150 years.

1923 – FLYING SCOTSMAN
Arguably the most famous locomotive in the world, Flying Scotsman became the first steam engine to officially clock 100mph.

1938 – MALLARD
The holder of the world speed record for steam locomotives for 75 years and counting, Mallard was designed by Sir Nigel Gresley as part of the A4 class. The 126mph record was achieved on July 3, 1938, on the slight downward grade of Stoke Bank south of Grantham on the East Coast Main Line, and the highest speed was recorded between Little Bytham and Essendine. Retired in 1963 after covering almost one and a half million miles, it is now a major attraction at the National Railway Museum in York.

"GRESLEY'S A4 CLASS, WITH THEIR STREAMLINED DESIGN, HAD A LONG DISTANCE, HIGH-SPEED CAPABILITY AND LOOKED LIKE NOTHING ELSE ON RAILS, BEFORE OR SINCE"

YOU don't have to be a railway enthusiast to name the two most famous steam locomotives in the world. Most people will respond with the answer Stephenson's Rocket and Flying Scotsman.

But many others will be able to add that there is a third member of this steaming holy trinity: Mallard. Not a bad reputation for a machine to enjoy more than three-quarters of a century after entering a world which has seen incredible changes in that time span.

If Rocket's claim to fame was its exceptional performance at the Rainhill Trials in 1829, leading to the success of the Liverpool and Manchester Railway (the world's first intercity passenger railway), then Mallard marked steam's zenith in attaining its world speed record of 126mph on July 3, 1938.

Rocket incorporated the basic concepts of the modern steam locomotive which were refined over the next 106 years, culminating in Sir Nigel Gresley's design for his A4 class, of which Mallard became the most famous member. What is fascinating is that the London & North Eastern Railway (LNER) was responsible for creating both Flying Scotsman and Mallard, a pair which became household names way ahead of locomotives built by Britain's other equally powerful pre-war private railway companies.

No 4472 Flying Scotsman achieved its celebrity both as the first steam locomotive to capture the official 100mph world speed record and then through savvy LNER marketing.

No 4468 Mallard and its A4 classmates are, in essence, the souped-up, go faster versions of Flying Scotsman and its brethren.

The A4 class, introduced in 1935 with their streamlined design, had a long distance, high-speed capability and looked like nothing else on the rails, before or since.

Looking fast even when at rest, their nicknames of "Streaks" was well deserved. Yet beneath the sleek panelling lies the kettle-like burblings, throaty animal roar and smoking emissions of a breathing steam locomotive, the nearest thing man has made to a living being, according to the late Rev Teddy Boston.

The 35-member class were built to haul express passenger trains on the LNER's East Coast Main Line from London (Kings Cross) via York and Newcastle to Edinburgh, Scotland.

They streaked up and down the East Coast until the early 1960s when they were superseded by the mighty Deltic diesel-electric locomotives.

Even then their day was not done and several A4s enjoyed an Indian summer until 1966 on the Scottish Region.

The A4s, therefore, can claim to have had a full 30 years in frontline express service, a record almost unsurpassed by any other steam locomotive class.

Craftsmen at Robert Stephenson and Co. complete a replica of Stephenson's Rocket for Henry Ford's transport museum in Detroit in 1929

IN THE BEGINNING...

OUR RAILWAY SYSTEM IS APPROPRIATELY DESCRIBED AS BRITAIN'S GREAT GIFT TO THE WORLD, BEING THE OLDEST ON THE PLANET.

"EARLY LOCOMOTIVES AND THEIR DESIGNERS STILL RESONATE TODAY"

Starting as a series of small, specialist lines spurred on by the mining industry to move its products, these isolated lines owned by small private railway companies were gradually connected together to create the incredible web of tracks across the country.

Such was their importance in driving the industrial revolution that the early locomotives and their designers still resonate today: Richard Trevithick's Pen-y-darren and Catch Me Who Can locomotives of 1802 and 1808, Matthew Murray's Salamanca of 1812, Hedley and Hackworth's Puffing Billy of 1814 and George Stephenson's Locomotion of 1825.

The big step changes came in 1825 with the Stephenson engineered Stockton & Darlington Railway, the world's first public steam railway, and in 1830 with his Liverpool & Manchester Railway, the world's first intercity passenger and freight line.

It's no surprise that these lines remained vitally important components of the two of the mighty big four companies created by government-forced amalgamations in 1923 – the London & North Eastern Railway and the London, Midland & Scottish respectively. ⊙

Top: A replica of Sans Pareil taking part in a re-enactment of the famous Rainhill Trials to mark the 150th anniversary of the event

Above: Liverpool & Manchester Centenary celebrations at Wavertree, Liverpool, organised by the London, Midland & Scottish Railway in 1930

Above right: George Stephenson, who is described as the 'Father of the Railways'

"CERTAIN SHINING EXAMPLES STOOD OUT"

Above: Locomotion No 1, with a replica of a Stockton & Darlington train behind, during the railway's centenary celebrations at Stockton on July 1, 1925

Left: George Stephenson's Killingworth Billy, which was built in 1826, ran on the Killingworth Railway until 1881. It is pictured here in 1945

Right: Liverpool and Manchester Railway's Lion steam locomotive, originally built in 1838, comes out of retirement to travel up and down the Rugby-Leamington line at Dunchurch, with driver and fireman both wearing period costume, in October 1961

The main competitors at Rainhill for the 1829 trails, courtesy of Rainhill Railway Museum

◎ Back in the 1840s, it was the railway mania which brought the national network into being with more than 6,000 miles of line, in spite of being proposed and operated by scores of rival companies.

Certain shining examples stood out. The multi-talented engineering genius Isambard Kingdom Brunel created the Great Western Railway from London to Bristol, starting in 1838. Ever the individual, he chose a broad gauge of seven feet and a quarter inch, which was too late an innovation and in 1892 it succumbed to the standard gauge of four feet and eight-and-a-half inches, which remains to this day in the UK and much of the world.

As with today's privatised network, during the 19th and 20th centuries companies inevitably amalgamated into bigger and more powerful groupings. The 19th century companies created some fantastic works of engineering which ◎

are still performing their original function today: Brunel's Box Tunnel (1841) and Royal Albert Bridge at Saltash (1859), Stephenson's Conwy railway bridge (1849), Fowler & Baker's Forth Bridge (1890).

Likewise, many of their great railway stations are still in use: London Paddington and King's Cross, Bristol Temple Meads, Glasgow Central, Liverpool Lime Street, Newcastle Central and York.

Rivalry was still intense but, as the railway consortia became better organised on the East Coast and West Coast Main Lines, they vied for traffic. Interestingly, the Midland Railway, a very well-founded concern built to get Midland's beer to the capital, was unable to partake in high-speed running as its route to Scotland was too circuitous, so it made comfort a selling point and greatly improved passenger conditions. ■

Top: **The footbridge at Birmingham New Street station at the turn of the 20th century**

Above: **A steam locomotive passing through Stephenson's Conwy railway bridge**

Right: **St John Ambulance volunteers and Royal Army Medical Corps officers await the return of war-wounded soldiers at Snow Hill railway station in Birmingham, circa 1916**

"MIDLAND RAILWAY MADE COMFORT A SELLING POINT AND GREATLY IMPROVED PASSENGER CONDITIONS"

"FANTASTIC WORKS OF ENGINEERING...

Below: Crowds gather at Paddington station prior to the next departure from platform five in August 1945

Liverpool Lime Street station in February 1953

Forth Bridge, which opened in 1890, connects Edinburgh to Fife. Below, workers admire the view after completing a 10-year repainting project

FATHER OF THE RAILWAYS

THE SON OF ILLITERATE PARENTS, GEORGE STEPHENSON WAS RESPONSIBLE FOR BUILDING THE WORLD'S FIRST STEAM-POWERED PUBLIC RAILWAY LINE.

Having paid to study at night school, George Stephenson was praised by the Victorian establishment as an example of "diligent application" with a "thirst for improvement".

Born in 1781 at Wylam, near Newcastle, he started work controlling pit winding gear but showed a natural expertise in maintaining colliery pumping gear and was soon promoted.

Richard Trevithick, credited with building the first locomotive in 1804, later constructed one on Tyneside. This inspired Stephenson to build Blucher, in 1814, for Killingworth Colliery.

This was the first successful flange-wheel adhesion locomotive – meaning its own weight gave enough grip to haul a train. The proposed Stockton & Darlington Railway planned to use horse-drawn carts but Stephenson persuaded its board to adopt steam power and surveyed the line in 1821, assisted by his 18-year-old son, Robert.

The Stephensons set up a locomotive works, Robert Stephenson & Co, in Newcastle

to make the motive power for the line, which was opened amid great fanfare in 1825.

Noting how even small inclines decelerated steam locomotives and declines rendered their brakes useless, George advocated level alignments.

He deployed this on engineering the Liverpool & Manchester Railway, necessitating his achievements of floating the line across the seemingly bottomless Chat Moss peat bog, building the Sankey viaduct and Rainhill skew arch bridge.

George, whose railway gauge of four feet and eight-and-a-half inches – allegedly based on the width of Roman chariot tracks – became the world's standard gauge, was besieged with work but after a decade his conservative views of engineering meant he was regarded as a safe pair of hands, rather than a pioneer.

He died in 1848 and the mantle of cutting-edge railway engineering passed to his only son, Robert, his pupil Joseph Locke and their friend, Isambard Kingdom Brunel.

...WHICH ARE STILL PERFORMING THEIR ORIGINAL FUNCTION TODAY"

1888

KEY DATES IN EPIC JOURNEY

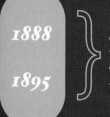

1888
1895
The passenger trains of rival companies would secretly race each other from London to Scotland

1896
1931
A West Coast overnight express derailed at excessive speed on curves at Preston. Journey times were later slowed to take a minimum time of eight hours

1932
Journey time restrictions were lifted, setting the stage for faster rail travel

RACE TO THE NORTH

In the late 19th century, the pace hotted up on the West and East Coasts, in what the press dubbed the "Race to the North", when especially in the summers of 1888 and 1895 passenger trains of the competing groups of companies would literally race each other from London to Scotland.

The railway companies hotly denied in public that any "races" were taking place but matters came to a head in July 1896 when a West Coast overnight express derailed at excessive speed on curves at Preston. One person was killed and the train was wrecked.

A public inquiry revealed neither driver of the double-headed train was trained for high-speed running.

As a matter of public reassurance, London to Edinburgh and Glasgow journey times were slowed to take a minimum time of eight hours.

Taking away any incentive to improve journey times, this cartel agreement unbelievably ran until the early 1930s.

Against this background, the stage was set for the streamlined-era trains to make such an impact – and the story that unfolds in these pages.

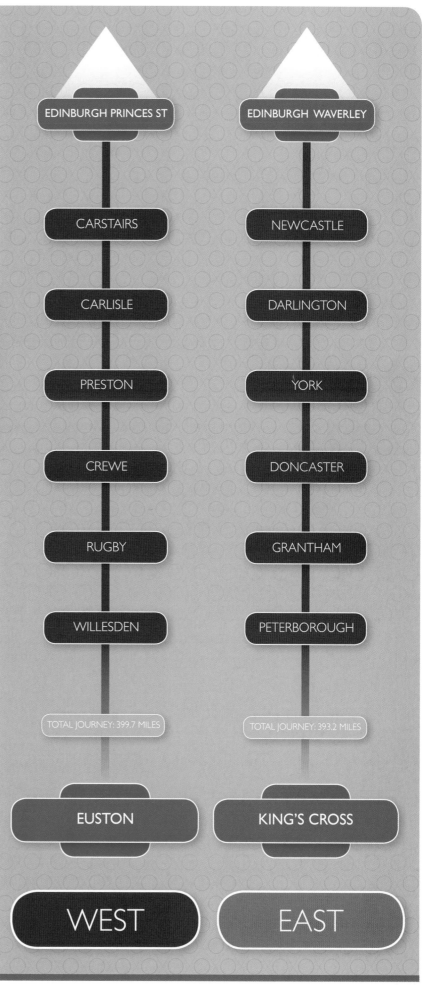

EDINBURGH PRINCES ST

CARSTAIRS

CARLISLE

PRESTON

CREWE

RUGBY

WILLESDEN

TOTAL JOURNEY: 399.7 MILES

EUSTON

WEST

EDINBURGH WAVERLEY

NEWCASTLE

DARLINGTON

YORK

DONCASTER

GRANTHAM

PETERBOROUGH

TOTAL JOURNEY: 393.2 MILES

KING'S CROSS

EAST

"THE STAGE WAS
SET FOR THE
STREAMLINED-
ERA TRAINS"

NEED FOR SPEED

THE DAWN OF THE STREAMLINED TRAIN HERALDED A GOLDEN AGE OF STEAM ON OUR RAILWAYS

"STREAMLINED DESIGN LOOKED MODERN AND FAST, EVEN WHEN AT A STANDSTILL, AND SUITED THE JAZZ AGE PERFECTLY"

Top: **A poster advertising the Silver Jubilee service in 1935**

Right: **A4 steam locomotive Sir Nigel Gresley, named after the engineer, stops at Newcastle Central Station on June 18, 1972, as part of the first East Coast Main Line steam rail tour in five years**

Speed, said the writer Aldous Huxley, provides the one genuinely modern pleasure.

Nothing better embodied this than the dawn of the streamlined train in Britain, the epitome of the golden age of steam on the railways between the wars.

It was a world with a mania for streamlined design to be applied to everything from jewellery to factory facades.

Streamlined design looked modern and fast, even when at a standstill, and suited the mood of the jazz age perfectly.

Britain's 1930s streamlined steam expresses complemented this mood to the maximum.

Not only did they look fast with their modernist art deco styling which was unlike any train seen before – they were fast, with their headline-grabbing runs.

First out the engine shed burst the London & North Eastern Railway's Silver Jubilee in 1935, hauled by the first of Sir Nigel Gresley's A4s, Silver Link.

Its innovative wedge-shaped outward appearance bore no resemblance to the preceding A3 class.

After handling the service for several weeks alone, Silver Link was joined by classmates Silver Fox, Silver King and Quicksilver.

This silver-grey arrow of the rails cut the London King's Cross - Newcastle journey time to just four hours, travelling at an average speed of 67mph. ⊙

"IT WAS A WORLD WITH A MANIA FOR STREAMLINED DESIGN TO BE APPLIED TO EVERYTHING FROM JEWELLERY TO FACTORY FACADES"

Top: In the 1930s, streamline design was all the rage, and was used to create this Royal Air Mail Service vehicle

Left: Inside the LNER Coronation train's observation car, pictured on April 13, 1945

Top left: The art deco style, as seen here on the Cunard liner Queen Mary in 1936, was used for the designs of the streamlined trains

Above: LNER's A4 class Silver King pictured in 1938

Bottom left: Passengers at their tables in a typical scene aboard a train during the 1930s

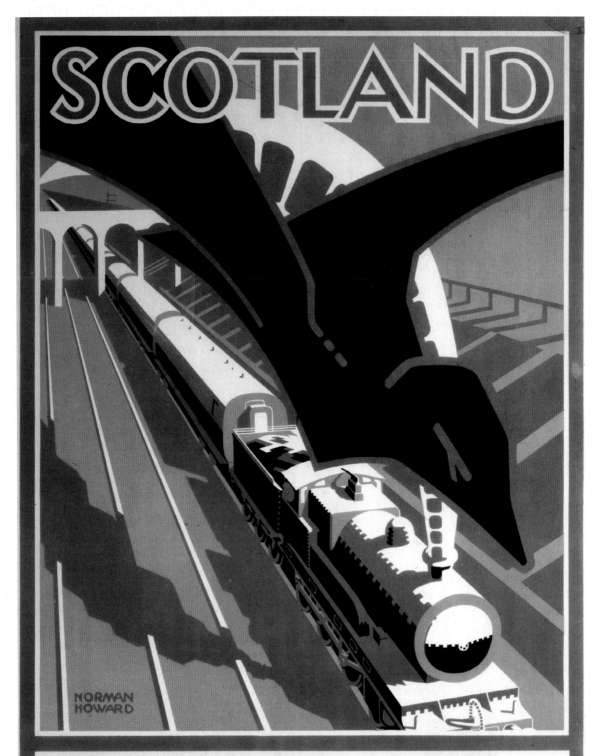

Progress Posters Nº 2.

STEAM!

THE "KING ARTHUR" CLASS, WEST OF ENGLAND EXPRESS

◄ 91 OF THE MOST POWERFUL ►
ENGINES ARE BEING DELIVERED
TO THE SOUTHERN RAILWAY THIS
SUMMER, COSTING OVER £600,000.

SOUTHERN

LONDON & NORTH EASTERN RAILWAY

SCARBOROUGH
IT'S QUICKER BY RAIL

SO SWIFTLY
HOME

by

SOUTHERN ELECTRIC

"THE CORONATION"
ON THE EAST COAST ENTERING SCOTLAND
IT'S QUICKER BY RAIL
FULL INFORMATION FROM ANY L·N·E·R OFFICE OR AGENCY

While streamlining could be dismissed as American marketing flim-flam foolishly imported to Britain, in fact it generated extra traffic for the railways and made money, at a time when managers were already anxious that they would soon lose passengers to embryonic air and road travel.

The Silver Jubilee was joined by The Coronation, in 1936, with its A4 locomotives named after dominions in the British Empire, of which Dominion of Canada and Union of South Africa survive.

The West Riding Limited followed in 1937, aimed at Yorkshire wool barons, with two dedicated A4s, Golden Fleece and Golden Shuttle. The latter was renamed Dwight D Eisenhower after the war and preserved at the US National Railroad Museum.

These glamorous high-speed trains with their spacious lounges, deluxe décor, cocktail bars and observation cars caught the public imagination and people wanted to travel (and be seen travelling) on them.

Top: A4 locomotive Dominon of Canada leaving London's King's Cross station for Edinburgh in June 1938

Right: A4 steam locomotive Dwight D. Eisenhower, which was originally known as Golden Shuttle but was renamed in 1946 in honour of the American wartime general

"SPACIOUS LOUNGES, DELUXE DÉCOR, COCKTAIL BARS AND OBSERVATION CARS"

Sir Nigel Gresley is photographed at the Doncaster Works with the A4 Pacific No 4498 he designed and which was named after him

THE Coronation Scot

EUSTON DEPART 1.30 P.M. | GLASGOW (CENTRAL) DEPART 1.30 P.M.
GLASGOW (CENTRAL) ARRIVE 8.0 P.M. | EUSTON ARRIVE 8.0 P.M.
COMMENCING JULY 5TH (MONDAYS TO FRIDAYS)

6½ HOURS

LONDON MIDLAND & SCOTTISH RAILWAY

A replica of Stephenson's Rocket is pictured in front of a locomotive built for the Coronation Scot service in May 1937

"THE OUTBREAK OF THE WAR PUT A SUDDEN STOP TO THESE ALL-TOO-BRIEF, BUT CAPTIVATING, ADVENTURES"

⊘ As a result, the London, Midland & Scottish Railway, operating the rival West Coast Main Line from London Euston to Glasgow, could not afford to be left behind and introduced its own streamliner, The Coronation Scot.

Powered by Sir William Stanier's new Princess Coronation class, the arrival of this blue-liveried train set the scene for the competing record-breaking runs between the capital and Scotland.

The Coronation Scot made such an impact that the composer Vivian Ellis wrote an orchestral piece of that name in celebration which became famous as the theme for BBC radio series Paul Temple. Yet behind the scenes was an incredible and all-too-familiar British effort of making the project happen against all the odds.

The trains were launched with fairly basic planning and although the steam locomotives themselves were very well designed, wood-framed rolling stock was built using traditional methods.

Before any of this could be rectified, the outbreak of the Second World War put a sudden and permanent stop to these all-too-brief, but captivating, adventures. ■

PROFILE OF A GENIUS

SIR NIGEL GRESLEY'S LOCOMOTIVES WERE NOT ONLY EXTREMELY POWERFUL MACHINES, THEY LOOKED SUPREMELY ELEGANT TOO

Born in Edinburgh in 1876, Sir Nigel Gresley was one of Britain's foremost steam locomotive engineers and his technical genius touched the creation of some of the most famous locomotives of all time.

These include the A1 (later A3) 4-6-2 pacific express class locomotive No 4472 Flying Scotsman and A4 class No 4468 Mallard.

His locomotives were not only powerful, functional and mechanically successful, they looked supremely elegant.

Although best associated with the Great Northern Railway and LNER at Doncaster from 1905, he served as an apprentice for the London & North Western Railway at Crewe and then moved to the Lancashire & Yorkshire Railway at Horwich and Newton Heath, Manchester.

Gresley was knighted for his services to the railway industry in 1936.

He died after a short illness on April 5, 1941, aged 64, and was buried in Netherseal, Derbyshire.

ROYAL
ORDER BRIDGE

"THE COR
CROSSING THE ROYAL BORDER
IT'S QUIC
FULL INFORMATION FROM

ONATION"
BRIDGE BERWICK-upon-TWEED
R BY RAIL
L·N·E·R OFFICE OR AGENCY

MALLARD
JULY 3, 1938

RECORD BREAKER

UNTIL THE MORNING OF JULY 3, 1938, GRESLEY A4 PACIFIC NO 4468 MALLARD APPEARED TO BE JUST ANOTHER MEMBER OF THE LNER'S NEW FRONTLINE EXPRESS PASSENGER LOCOMOTIVE FLEET. HOWEVER, ALL WAS NOT QUITE WHAT IT SEEMED.

> "THE WESTINGHOUSE TEAM WERE ONLY TOLD THE TRUE PURPOSE OF THE TRIP AFTER THE TRAIN'S NORTHBOUND RUN"

Left: **Mallard on Sunday, July 3, 1938 at Barkston on the East Coast Main Line just before it set off on its record-breaking run**

Mallard was built in March 1938 with the new Kylchap double chimney and blastpipe to improve steaming. Wind tunnel tests on a Plasticine model of the A4 to improve smoke dispersal struck lucky when, by chance, an indented thumb print behind the chimney did the trick.

Behind all this frenetic activity was the desire to beat not only the rival LMS and its chief mechanical engineer Sir William Stanier's 114mph British record but also the Germans, whose DRG Class 5 002 had reached 124.5mph, a world-record speed for a steam locomotive, in 1936.

To go faster you also need to have better braking and Gresley decided to trial the Westinghouse braking system as used by the rival LMS, and the record run was effectively done under the cover of the Westinghouse brake trials.

He chose driver Joe Duddington, 61, for the East Coast Main Line run, a man who pushed engines hard and had a fondness for Mallard.

Fireman Thomas Bray had also known Mallard since its building and was experienced in handling the A4s.

Gresley, 61, by now was not a well man and in fact missed the great day, asking his technical assistant Norman Newsome to make the arrangements.

The footplate crew and the Westinghouse team were only told the true purpose of the trip after the train's northbound run from Wood Green, in north London, to Barkston near Grantham.

The Westinghouse men were offered a taxi back but everyone elected to stay on the train for the record attempt. ⊙

In spite of an initial speed restriction on the southbound run, Mallard accelerated up Stoke Bank at 85mph, hitting 113mph at the summit, 6mph faster than classmate Silver Fox's record.

Racing down Stoke Bank the dynamometer car behind the loco recorded 120mph, thereby officially breaking the LMS' record with its No 6220 Coronation.

However, there were still a few minutes before the crew had to slow for the Essendine curves and they accelerated the train even more.

For a quarter of a mile the dynamometer car confirmed the train was travelling at 126mph. By now the German record was also broken forever.

It has been claimed the train had rocked so violently that the dining car crockery smashed and red-hot, bullet-like flying cinders from Mallard apparently broke windows at Little Bytham station, although some said the train ran very smoothly. The braking force caused Mallard's big end bearing to run hot. Slow, not fast, running was in order to reach Peterborough safely without the locomotive being written off.

Ironically, a much older Ivatt Atlantic – a class superseded by the A4s – pulled the train back to King's Cross.

It didn't detract from the overall news blitz. The national newspapers had been tipped off about the record-breaking run and nicknamed Mallard the "Blue Streak".

Driver Duddington and Fireman Bray received a tumultuous welcome in London, becoming heroes in Britain and abroad.

Yet the day after their astonishing achievement they were back on the footplate for another ordinary day at work. ■

Above: **Members of the crew reflect on their achievement following Mallard's record-breaking run**

Right: **Mallard's cab interior, showing the firebox, pressure gauges, boiler and dials**

"DRIVER DUDDINGTON AND FIREMAN BRAY RECEIVED A TUMULTUOUS WELCOME IN LONDON, BECOMING HEROES IN BRITAIN AND ABROAD"

Mallard, with the dynamometer
car behind the tender, on the day
of the historic run. For a quarter
of a mile the dynamometer car
confirmed the locomotive was
travelling at 126mph

PUSHING IT TO THE LIMIT

DRIVER JOE DUDDINGTON WAS 61 WHEN HE WAS HAND-PICKED BY SIR NIGEL GRESLEY HIMSELF FOR THE SECRET ATTEMPT AT THE WORLD SPEED RECORD

Joe Duddington had perfect credentials for driving the Mallard for its record-breaking run attempt.

He was renowned for taking calculated risks and pushing engines to their limits.

Duddington also had a fondness in particular for Mallard ("my lovely blue engine") since it was rolled out of Doncaster works when new in March 1938.

Fireman Thomas Bray had also known Mallard since its building and was experienced in handling the A4s. Bray had the crucial combination of being able to shovel coal fast and the

stamina to do it for a long time.

Bob Gwynne, associate curator of rail vehicles at the National Railway Museum, said: "Duddington, then aged 61, climbed into the cab, turned his cap around – as had George Formby in the 1935 film No Limit – and drove Mallard into the history books.

"He had 27 years on the footplate, and had once driven the Scarborough Flyer for 144 miles at over 74mph (average speed), considered at the time to be the highest speed ever maintained by steam in the UK."

"DUDDINGTON WAS RENOWNED FOR TAKING CALCULATED RISKS AND PUSHING ENGINES TO THEIR LIMITS"

A painting by Gerald Coulson, on display at the National Railway Museum, of Mallard breaking the world speed record

I t was the fastest steam-powered rail journey of all time – but news of the full scale of Mallard's achievement travelled at a far slower pace.

The record-breaking run was featured on Page 2 of the Daily Mirror on July 4, 1938. However, the speed was slightly under-estimated at the time, and it was not until after Sir Nigel Gresley's death in 1941 that it was widely agreed 126mph had been reached.

The world record was also wrongly credited to the Americans. Mallard was acknowledged only to have broken the British record – despite there being no official confirmation of the 127mph run that Pennsylvania Railroad's S1 prototype was said to have achieved.

In contrast, Mallard's record run was confirmed by technical recording equipment in the dynamometer car behind the engine. Plaques were affixed to each side of the locomotive commemorating the feat in 1948.

David Morgan, the former editor of US Trains magazine, was quoted in the Journal of the Stephenson Locomotive Society (January 1980) as saying: "I'm afraid that you'll not find authenticated records covering maximum speeds attained by Pennsylvania Railroad's 6100 (S1) or its related T1 duplex-drive machine.

"Train timing on this side of the Atlantic is simply not of the quality or quantity you are familiar with in the UK or on the Continent."

The stories featured alongside Mallard in the Daily Mirror also offer a fascinating insight into the news of the day.

The death of a British student who fell from a third-floor window was being investigated in France, while in New York a young man was arrested at Long Beach promenade, Long Island, for the crime of wearing braces – which were barred from the resort.

And in the days before sport news was mostly reserved for the back pages, the paper highlighted the criticism aimed at Helen Moody for her alleged lack of sportsmanship as she beat her injury-stricken opponent in the Wimbledon tennis final, while spectacled cricketer Paul Gibb was set to make his England debut against Australia. ■

Right: **Page 2 of the Daily Mirror on July 4, 1938**

BRITAIN'S FASTEST EVER EXPRESS DOES 125 MILES AN HOUR

A SPEED of 125 m.p.h.—nearly eleven miles an hour over the previous British record for steam locomotives—was reached yesterday by an L.N.E.R. Coronation streamlined express, the Mallard, on a test run between Grantham and Peterborough.

World record for steam locomotives is claimed by America with 127 m.p.h.

Mallard was driven by Driver J. Duddington and Fireman T. H. Bray, of Doncaster, and Locomotive Inspector J. Jenkins, of London, was also on the footplate.

The locomotive was drawing a streamlined train to which was attached a dynamometer car, in which were charts and instruments which confirmed the record.

Passengers were a party of engineers.

The maximum speed was maintained for 306 yards near Little Bytham Station, and was reduced only because of the approaching junction at Essendine.

Previously in the run a speed of 120 m.p.h. had been maintained for approximately three miles.

Mallard is one of the type of streamlined Pacific locomotives designed by Sir Nigel Gresley, chief mechanical engineer of the L.N.E.R. It was built at Doncaster Works in March and is stationed at Doncaster.

The previous British record-holder was the L.M.S. Coronation Scot, which, on its inaugural run on June 29 last year, driven by Tom Clarke, of Crewe, reached 114 m.p.h.

Although unable to secure the world record for steam trains, Britain holds the record for the highest sustained speed—an average of 100 m.p.h. for nearly forty-three miles, set up by the engine Silver Link, drawing the Silver Jubilee train on a test run in 1935.

Secrets Case No. 2

While the Government Official Secrets case rocks Britain, Chesham (Bucks) Urban Council have their own official inquiry—to trace the source of a leakage of Council business.

A townsman has written to Mr. Geoffrey O. Bell, the chairman, alleging that committee matters which have leaked may harm his business.

The chairman has obtained a signed statement from Council officials that they have not disclosed information. Councillors have also given denials.

Says Mr. Bell: "We cannot do anything until we know the source of the leakage. I cannot say anything more at this stage without further leakage."

ENGLAND'S STUMPER HAS SPECS

ENGLAND will have a spectacled wicketkeeper in the *Third Test*, which begins at Old Trafford, Manchester, on Friday.

He is Paul Gibb, twenty-five, a Cambridge Blue and Yorkshire county player.

Gibb is among the thirteen chosen yesterday at a 500-year-old inn at Gloucester. He comes into the team in place of Leslie Ames (Kent), who is injured.

Smailes, the Yorkshire bowler, who took six Australian wickets for 92 at Sheffield on Saturday, is included. So is Goddard, the Gloucestershire bowler.

Surprises are the selection of Nichols, the Essex fast bowler, and the dropping of Kenneth Farnes, of the same club.

"I am glad Nichols has been chosen. He is a magnificent bowler and a tremendous trier," said Farnes yesterday.

Team and comments—Page 26.

FOREST TRUNK CRIME

Two youths on their way to Whipps Cross Lido, Epping Forest, yesterday found a large suitcase, inside which was the body of a few-months-old male child. A piece of string was found its neck.

POLICE ARE PROBING BRITON'S DEATH FALL

BY A SPECIAL CORRESPONDENT

ON the third floor of a house in Rue Andrioli, Nice, a window burst open.

Down on to the pavement crashed a young student, an Englishman—John Bennett, of Lyndhurst, Hants. An hour later he died in hospital without having uttered a word.

He had fallen from the window of a flat. In it there had been four other people—a doctor of science, Erich Rigby, aged twenty-nine; his blonde wife, Dauphine, twenty-one; his sister, Enid, twenty-three, and a friend, Mario Naldi-Dini, a musician.

For eight hours they were questioned by the French police. Every moment of their day of merry holidaymaking in Riviera resorts was accounted for.

Bennett, aged twenty-three, son of a well-known cotton broker, had been for some time in a Monte Carlo hospital. He had telephoned Dr. Rigby asking him to take him out for a day.

The five made a dinner party at a Monte Carlo restaurant.

Later they returned to Nice and went to several night clubs. There they had drinks. About four o'clock Dr. Rigby suggested they should go home and that Mr. Bennett should stay with him, as it was too late for him to go back to the Monte Carlo hospital.

"We had very few drinks," Dr. Rigby told me to-day, "but when we came into the air they seemed to have affected Bennett."

"He Was Not There—"

"When we arrived at our flat my wife and I went straight to our bedroom. My sister stayed in another room with Naldi-Dini, finishing their English-French lesson, as they always did.

"I had put Mr. Bennett in a third room. Soon after I was in bed I heard him moving about.

"I got up and I found him in the hall. He wanted a drink. I told him there was nothing to drink and to go back to bed.

"Bennett returned to his room. There I could hear him mumbling to himself. I got up again and looked for him.

"It was then that I heard him near the window. I looked into his room, but he was not there. I then walked into the other room, but it was empty.

"I had a premonition, and looked out of the window. There was Bennett lying on the pavement below.

"I put on a robe and rushed downstairs. There was nothing I could do. He died shortly after he arrived at the hospital.

"We were good friends, and he and his father, Humphrey Bennett, of Yew Tree Cottage, Emery Down, Lyndhurst (Hants), was associated with me in a new company backing a recording machine I have invented."

The police are inclined to believe it was an accident.

Bennett's father told the *Daily Mirror*:—"John had been holidaymaking on the Continent for some months. He wanted to obtain a wider knowledge of the world."

Mr. Sinclair Hill, the film producer, said John was assistant director of a number of famous films, including "Hyde Park Corner," "Gay Adventure," Claude Hulbert's "Take a Chance" and "Command Performance."

GOLD LINER SPRINGS LEAK

The Cunard-White Star liner Ascania, which went aground in the St. Lawrence River on Saturday, was last night leaking in her forward holds.

Barges carrying 100 longshoremen are on their way from Quebec to lighten the cargo, which includes £600,000 worth of gold.

TWO HELENS ARE "MUSCLE MOLLS," SAY U.S. WRITERS

FROM OUR OWN CORRESPONDENT
NEW YORK (Sunday).

BITTER comments appear in the American Press to-day on yesterday's match at Wimbledon between Helen Wills Moody and Helen Jacobs.

In the *New York Mirror* columnist Consadine reports:—"Although Jacobs was suffering badly from an injury, Moody drives onwards, relentlessly chasing her opponent back and forth against the court with sizzling, angled drives."

Comments Consadine:—

"Ah, those dear muscle molls of sport. In them must burn only the killer instinct."

"Moody triumphs in feud of Helens," reads huge headlines in the *New York Sunday News*, and sports editor Jimmy Powers writes: "Moody better player. Jacobs better sport."

"Sportsmanship?"

Another column headed "Sportsmanship" reads:—

"Many people shook their heads. Mrs. Moody's actions were not their ideas of sportsmanship."

A writer in the *Times* calls it "Grudge fight," pointing out that the two Helens did not exchange a single smile or remark until the match ran out, when they shook hands at the end.

"Something more gallant in Jacobs losing than in Moody winning," says *New York Morning Telegraph*.

A.R.P. WAGE DEMAND THREAT TO ENTIRE SYSTEM

TRADE Unionists in Plymouth have taken a stand that may wreck the national scheme of Air Raid Precautions work. In an official letter to the Plymouth Air Raid Precautions Committee, the local trade unions state that they consider their members should be paid for their A.R.P. work.

"Gravest Concern"

Alderman Solomon Stephens, Lord Mayor of Plymouth and chairman of the A.R.P. Committee, told the *Daily Mirror* last night:—

"The attitude of the trade unions has given us the gravest concern. To pay for this work is completely contradictory to the whole idea of the voluntary spirit in A.R.P. work.

"I cannot over-emphasise the seriousness of their attitude, and if the idea spreads nationally, it may damage the whole A.R.P. scheme."

HOW MALLARD BECAME STEAM'S SPEED MACHINE

A FRENCH DESIGNER, THE STREAMLINED BUGATTI RAILCAR AND A DOUBLE CHIMNEY ALL PLAYED A PART IN HELPING A4 LOCOMOTIVE RACE ITS WAY INTO THE RECORD BOOKS

Mallard was the 28th of the 35 A4 class of express locomotives designed by Sir Nigel Gresley, ordered from LNER's Doncaster railway works in November 1936 and completed on March 3, 1938, at a cost of £8,500.

In construction it was given special consideration including modifications gained through experience of its classmates.

In particular, it received a Kylchap double chimney and blastpipe.

The A4 class has a pacific wheel arrangement of 4-6-2, which is defined as four bogie wheels supporting the front end and smokebox, six driving wheels (6ft 8ins diameter) and two trailing wheels, supporting the firebox and cab.

An integral part of the design was the eight-wheeled tender coupled behind the locomotive, carrying the water and nine tonnes of coal.

For the high-speed regular train services, Gresley had designed a special corridor tender, which uniquely allowed the crew access to the train behind, so they could be relieved on long runs. The A4s were aerodynamic

from top to bottom, which means that their streamlining was integral to the design, not least in its ability to carry smoke clear of the locomotive, a vital consideration and never more than at high speed.

Gresley was inspired by how the Bugatti streamlined petrol railcars pushed the air upwards instead of sideways. Unlike other streamlined classes, the A4s were never 'defrocked' and rebuilt with a more traditional appearance.

Although based on Gresley's A3 class (of which Flying Scotsman is its most famous and sole remaining example), the boiler pressure was increased to 250lbs per square inch from 180psi, and the boiler at 18ft long, was made a foot shorter than their older brethren. The three cylinders were also made slightly smaller.

Influenced by the great French railway designer Andre Chapelon, Gresley crucially also streamlined the inside workings of the A4s, as they were to operate at their maximum above 75mph – the opposite of usual practice when hauling heavy trains.

Painting by Phil Belbin

HAVE YOU EVER WONDERED WHAT IT WAS LIKE TO BE ON BOARD MALLARD AS IT BROKE THE WORLD SPEED RECORD?

At the National Railway Museum, you can experience the sights, sounds and smells of the world's fastest steam locomotive on a thrilling simulator ride.

The state-of-the-art Mallard Experience, pictured left, uses a high definition, animated film to recreate the record-breaking run down Stoke Bank.

Meet the people who were part of this amazing journey as driver Joe Duddington, fireman Tom Bray and

inspector Sam Jenkins are digitally recreated to reprise their roles of the day.

For those who wish to enjoy the experience without motion, there is also a static version available, as well as a ride for the under-fives.

This Mallard Experience is located in the Great Hall and costs £5 for adults and £4 for children. Images courtesy of Metropolis.

DYNAMOMETER CAR INTERIOR VIEW

"EXPERIENCE THE SIGHTS, SMELLS AND SOUNDS OF THE WORLD'S FASTEST STEAM LOCOMOTIVE"

TRAVELLING THROUGH STOKE TUNNEL

THE WAR YEARS

THE GLAMOUR OF THE STREAMLINED SERVICES WERE OBVIOUSLY INCOMPATIBLE WITH THE PRIORITIES OF WARTIME. AS IF A HARBINGER OF WHAT WAS TO COME, THE FINAL STREAMLINED SERVICES OPERATED ON AUGUST 31, 1939, THREE DAYS BEFORE THE SECOND WORLD WAR BEGAN

Above: **Women did men's jobs during the Second World War, including this railway porter**

Above right: **These women are busy cleaning a steam locomotive in 1941**

The Emergency Powers (Defence) Act of 1939 enabled services to be drastically pruned while evacuation and troop trains were introduced.

Gradually, passenger services resumed but were timetabled at much lower speeds, with blackouts imposed at night-time, and were of secondary importance to freight. Maintenance was cut back, with a consequent suffering in the standards of track, motive power and rolling stock.

As the A4s were regarded as unsuited to the newly-imposed wartime austerity, King's Cross shed mothballed its allocation. Soon, though, the national emergency demanded that all motive power was mobilised for the war effort and the entire class were at work again. Instead of pulling light, seven-coach high-speed trains, they were hauling extremely heavy, 20-coach trains entirely at odds with their original purpose. It says much for the soundness of Gresley and his team's ⊙

"INSTEAD OF PULLING LIGHT, SEVEN-COACH HIGH-SPEED TRAINS, THEY WERE HAULING EXTREMELY HEAVY, 20-COACH TRAINS"

Left: Large crowds at Paddington station ready to rush off to the coast on a bank holiday weekend in 1941. However, some resorts were banned, including Margate, Southend and Brighton, and holidaymakers were turned back by military police, causing huge delays. Resorts outside the military defence zone were full to capacity and beyond

A Japanese family leaving Euston station to return home to Japan in June 1940

Passengers at Paddington
station having their ID cards
checked by the police and army
in 1945

design that these locomotives were such a success in this unexpectedly new but vital role.

One obvious change caused by wartime conditions was the removal of the aerofoil-shaped metal skirts, or valances, over the driving wheels for ease of maintenance.

This change instantly diminished the locomotive's art deco-style looks but, with their driving wheels and motion exposed, it gave them a much beefier, more powerful appearance.

Bizarrely, the A4s' mellifluous chime whistles were also removed in 1942 and melted down as it was thought they might be confused with air raid sirens.

New chime whistles were substituted after the war.

Below: **Child evacuees leave Euston and head for safer parts of the country in 1939**

"BIZARRELY, THE A4s' MELLIFLUOUS CHIME WHISTLES WERE ALSO REMOVED IN 1942 AND MELTED DOWN AS IT WAS THOUGHT THEY MIGHT BE CONFUSED WITH AIR RAID SIRENS"

⊙ The unluckiest A4 was No 4469 Sir Ralph Wedgwood, which was so severely damaged during a Baedeker air raid in April 1942 on York that it was scrapped.

The locomotive was in the York shed which is now the National Railway Museum and a plaque on the Great Hall's floor marks the site.

As for the streamlined trains, they too were wartime victims and never re-emerged in the era of peacetime austerity where moving the masses was the priority, not pandering to the posh few. ■

Top: **Two women look after the railway signals at Warmsworth, near Doncaster, in 1941**

Right: **Women railway porters at Crewe station in 1941**

Railway workers clean
out a steam engine
boiler in 1942

Above: **A railway inspector and women cleaners
working on an engine in the floodlit pit of a train
shed in 1944**

"THE UNLUCKIEST
A4 WAS NO 4469 SIR
RALPH WEDGWOOD,
WHICH WAS SO
SEVERELY DAMAGED
DURING A BAEDEKER
AIR RAID IN APRIL 1942"

The Silver Jubilee locomotive as it looked in 1944

A steam engine is given the cleaning treatment in 1941

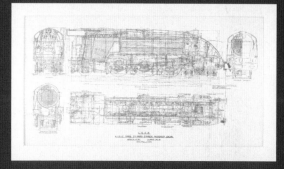

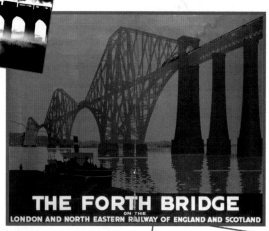

END OF THE LINE

WITH WAR OVER, THE A4 ENGINES CARRIED ON AS THE PREMIER FRONTLINE EXPRESS MOTIVE POWER ON THE EAST COAST MAIN LINE IN THE LONG, SLOW RETURN TO NORMAL PEACETIME LIFE.

Above: The Commonwealth of Australia steam locomotive, pictured in Newcastle in the mid-1950s

Right: Steam locomotive Sir Nigel Gresley alongside a Brush Type 4 diesel locomotive on September 7, 1975

"DIESEL AND ELECTRIC POWER WERE CLEARLY EMERGING AS THE FUTURE MOTIVE POWER"

In spite of the maintenance backlog and nationalisation putting the emphasis on railways as being foremost a public service, there was clearly an appetite for one last hurrah from the steam camp. And the A4s, well into their second decade, were critical to its success.

Diesel and electric power were clearly emerging as the future motive power, already demonstrating their prowess in the US and making steady headway in mainland Europe.

Instead of the pre-war lightweight streamlined trains, the newly-formed British Railways decided upon a steam-hauled heavy daily summer service running non-stop between London King's Cross and Edinburgh, starting in 1949. Initially called the Capitals Limited, it became better known as The Elizabethan, renamed in honour of ⊙

Queen Elizabeth II's accession to the throne in 1953.

Running the 393 miles in six-and-a-half hours, it was the world's longest non-stop scheduled railway service.

The average speed of a shade over 60mph and punctuality was a fine achievement given the railway's poor state of infrastructure at that time.

The train was immortalised in a 1954 British Transport Film called, appropriately, Elizabethan Express. Made as a promotional film, now it is hailed as a memorable retrospective of British Railways' halcyon days of steam.

Far left: A journalist interviewing a train driver at King's Cross station in 1952. Silver Fox was hauling a Capitals Limited train as part of a non-stop summertime service from London to Edinburgh

Left: The Elizabethan travelling through Newcastle Central Station on June 30, 1953

Below: The Elizabethan at speed on January 10, 1956, headed by Class A4 locomotive Gannet on the longest non-stop run in the world, from London to Edinburgh

"A4 CLASS NO 60017 SILVER FOX IS VERY MUCH STAR OF THE FILM, WITH MAGNIFICENT FOOTAGE OF THE LOCOMOTIVE IN ACTION"

A4 class No 60017 Silver Fox is very much the star of the film with magnificent footage of the locomotive in action and the crew battling to keep the train on time.

The Elizabethan service lasted until 1963. The honour fell to Mallard to power the very last steam-hauled northbound (or "down") Elizabethan on September 8, 1961.

Ironically, the Deltic diesels which replaced the A4s could not change crew while moving and therefore had to stop at York, undermining The Elizabethan's non-stop purpose, although overall journey times were still quicker.

Above: No 60017 locomotive Silver Fox pictured in 1955

A train driver and fireman are pictured on a steam locomotive footplate in 1956

DRIVER
P.E.HEAVENS.

600

RA 9

An Imperial Airways
plane flies over
Flying Scotsman in
Hertfordshire on
February 13, 1934

"COMPETITION FROM ROAD AND AIR TRAVEL WAS BECOMING A REALITY"

⊚ As the East Coast Main Line was upgraded in the 1950s, other expresses emerged with the A4s in charge, such as the Tees-Tyne Pullman and White Rose which filled the former streamliner schedules. By now the competition from road and air travel was becoming a reality and an attempt was made to glamorise these expresses with names such as The Talisman and The Fair Maid. These evocative titles were slowly dispensed with after the age of steam as faster diesel trains dispensed with the need for special expresses.

In 1963, after covering almost one and a half million miles over a period of 25 years, Mallard was withdrawn from service. ■

Top: **Guard Henry Crossland blows his whistle and flags away Oliver Cromwell, the last steam locomotive to haul a mainline passenger service, as it leaves Manchester for Carlisle on August 11, 1968**

Above left: **A railwayman attaching the nameplate to an A4 loco Quicksilver, which was pulling The Fair Maid service in September 1957.**

Left: **Evening Star, the last steam locomotive to be built for British Railways, pulls in to Oxenhope station during the Worth Valley Railway's annual open day for enthusiasts in December 1982**

No.4472 Flying Scotsman at railway sidings in Shildon on August 22, 1975

Right: A driver is pictured on the footplate of an A4 locomotive in 1956

"THE DELTIC DIESELS WHICH REPLACED THE A4s COULD NOT CHANGE CREW WHILE MOVING AND THEREFORE HAD TO STOP AT YORK"

Mallard after it was withdrawn from service in 1963

Left: **Western Region train driver Reg Deacon and fireman Fred Phillips on the footplate of their loco, No. 7001 Sir James Milne, as it gathers speed through the suburbs of London in March 1950**

"OTHER EXPRESSES EMERGED WITH THE A4s IN CHARGE, SUCH AS THE TYNE-TEES PULLMAN AND WHITE ROSE"

Below: **Simmering in a shed yard, Mallard gets a check from its crew in March 1963, just prior to withdrawal by British Railways after 1.5 million miles of service**

MALLARD'S JOURNEY GOES ON

IT MAY HAVE BEEN WITHDRAWN FROM SERVICE IN 1963 BUT ENTHUSIASTS ENSURED THE HISTORIC LOCO WOULD NEVER BE FORGOTTEN

As the unsurpassed steam speed record holder, Mallard was chosen over A4 doyenne Silver Link for preservation and was cosmetically restored for pride of place in the British Museum of Transport, at Clapham, south London.

Moved to the newly-opened National Railway Museum in 1975 as a static exhibit, Mallard was restored to working order for the 50th speed record anniversary in 1988 but only operated a handful of York - Scarborough and York - Harrogate/Leeds passenger specials, as well as services to Carlisle and London Marylebone, plus a Post Office and BR Travellers Fayre dining car charters.

In July 2008, Mallard was displayed outside the museum with the three other UK residing A4s. This event has since been trumped for the 75th anniversary with the arrival of its two North American classmates this year for the Great Gathering of all six class members.

"MALLARD WAS RESTORED TO WORKING ORDER FOR THE 50TH SPEED RECORD ANNIVERSARY"

Above: **Mallard**
back in action after
being restored
to working order
for the 1988 speed
record anniversary
celebrations

Left: **Restoration**
work under way on
Mallard in 1985

Right: **The A4**
locomotives gathered
at the National
Railway Museum for
the 50th anniversary
celebrations.
Pictured are Mallard,
Bittern (disguised
as No 2509 Silver
Link) and Sir Nigel
Gresley

Chris Cade, from Platform 4 Theatre, dressed as Sir Nigel Gresley as he poses with Mallard at the National Railway Museum

GREAT GATHERING

THE REUNION OF MALLARD AND ITS SURVIVING SISTER LOCOS ATTRACTED TENS OF THOUSANDS OF PEOPLE TO THE NATIONAL RAILWAY MUSEUM IN YORK.

How do you celebrate the 75th anniversary of the fastest steam locomotive in the world, with its unbroken speed record?

For the 50th anniversary, Mallard itself was restored to working order but this was regarded as unfeasible to do again, so what next?

The answer couldn't have been bolder, thanks to the visionary thinking by the former director of the National Railway Museum, Steve Davies. He had the spine-tingling idea of bringing all six surviving members of the A4 class together at the NRM for what became known as the Great Gathering, with the Prince of Wales as patron.

Brilliant – except for one, not-so-small, detail. Two of the locomotives were preserved deep in North America: Dwight D Eisenhower had gone to the US National Railroad Museum, Wisconsin, and Dominion of Canada was shipped to the Exporail, the Canadian Railway Museum. ⊘

> "STEVE HAD THE SPINE-TINGLING IDEA OF BRINGING ALL SIX SURVIVING MEMBERS OF THE A4 CLASS TOGETHER AT THE NRM"

Railway enthusiasts arrive at the Great Gathering of the six remaining A4 class locomotives at the National Railway Museum

Keith and Kay Wood, from Boston, Lincolnshire, queue to board Mallard

"THE CHANCES OF SEEING THE HALF-DOZEN SURVIVORS TOGETHER AGAIN IN THE UK WAS UNIMAGINABLE AND IMPOSSIBLE"

Above: **Ron Birch, a former driver and fireman on Mallard, is pictured sitting inside the cab of the locomotive**

So it was a universally accepted truth amongst the rail preservation fraternity that the chances of seeing the half-dozen survivors together again in the UK was unimaginable and impossible.

Of course, scheduling the UK-based A4 quartet – Mallard, Bittern, Sir Nigel Gresley and Union of South Africa – to meet was the relatively easy part. It was nothing compared to the negotiations, removals and travel logistics by rail and sea of bringing the North American duo to Liverpool and then by road to the NRM's sites in York and Locomotion, Shildon, for cosmetic restoration. For example, Eisenhower was practically bricked into its shed and had to be inched out sideways by the contractor Moveright International. Dominion of Canada was lost for five days on the Canadian railway network and only located when a rail fan e-mailed a picture of it in a freight yard! Paperwork was mislaid. These and other delays meant the locomotives missed the original sailing date before finally arriving in Liverpool on October 3, 2012.

WHAT THEY SAID ABOUT GRESLEY'S A4 MASTERPIECES...

"Sir Nigel Gresley designed his A4 with the speed of a greyhound and the strength of a boar"

Paul Le Saux, Elizabethan Express, British Transport Film, 1954

"Shooting and winding through the countryside like a silver snake"

Newspaper report on the new Silver Jubilee express hauled by A4 class Silver Link, 1935

"They're marvellous engines all right, and they ride very nicely"

Driver Hutchinson, at Edinburgh after arrival with first northbound Coronation express, from London, July 1937

Mallard is "an example of British ingenuity"

Institution of Mechanical Engineers

"THEY ARE ONCE-IN-A-LIFETIME EVENTS AND PROBABLY WILL NEVER HAPPEN AGAIN"

The Dominion of Canada upon arriving in Liverpool, right, and, below, how it now looks after being repainted into its original garter blue colour, with a valanced single chimney, complete with Canadian bell and chime whistle and replica cabside crests

Top: Visitors at the Great Gathering event take pictures of Mallard and Dominion of Canada

Above: Tim Godfrey, left, the grandson of Sir Nigel Gresley, and Peter Townend, former shed master at King's Cross, stand in front of Mallard as they pose for the camera

⊙ Even though the Great Gatherings are now a reality, they are once-in-a-lifetime events and probably will never happen again, as the two North American A4s will return home early in 2014.

On June 29, 2013, the sixth and final A4 arrived in style for the event when No 4464 Bittern reached York with the Ebor Streak express charter from King's Cross, having attained a preservation speed record of 92.6mph on its journey.

Rock star and railway enthusiast Rod Stewart pulled a lever while appearing on BBC TV's One Show to turn Bittern around on the NRM's turntable and take its place in the A4 line-up.

The Great Gathering officially began on July 3, 2013, 75 years to the day that Mallard was immortalised with its dash down Stoke Bank, near Grantham. The Canadian High Commissioner Gordon Campbell unveiled the newly-restored Dominion of Canada, with Tim Godfrey, grandson of Sir Nigel Gresley, also present.

Opening the event, NRM director Paul Kirkman described it as "an international family reunion", thanks to the co-operation of three great national railway museums. ⊙

He added that the amazing sight had drawn people together from all over the world and, paying tribute to his predecessor, said: "I acknowledge the vision of the former director of the NRM, Steve Davies. I hope we have successfully delivered (his) dream and the dream of rail enthusiasts across the globe."

An astonishing 13,000 people visited the NRM on the first Saturday (10,000 more than usual). In all, nearly 140,000 visitors attended over 15 days, including a private visit from Prince Charles.

The event is repeated at York, on October 26 – November 8, 2013, and finally at the NRM's satellite museum, Locomotion, at Shildon, Co Durham, for the Great Goodbye, on February 15-23, 2014. ■

"THE AMAZING SIGHT HAD DRAWN PEOPLE TOGETHER FROM ALL OVER THE WORLD"

The Prince of Wales hopped on board Mallard, top, during his visit to the National Railway Museum in York to mark the Great Gathering celebrations

GREAT
GATHERING

Great Hall
National Railway Museum
York

MALLARD 75

MALLARD

NO 4468 (1938-63)

*Owned and based at National Railway Museum and on static display
(operational during 1986-8), in LNER blue livery.*

BITTERN

NO 4464 (1937-66)

*Based at Southall Railway Centre, owned by Jeremy Hosking and approved for
mainline use, in LNER blue livery.*

DOMINION OF CANADA

NO 4489 (1937-65)

*Owned and based at Exporail, the Canadian Railway Museum, Montreal, on static
display, in LNER blue livery (currently in UK for Mallard 75 celebration in 2013).
Originally built for the Coronation streamliner service.*

SIR NIGEL GRESLEY

NO 60007 (1937-66)

Based at North Yorkshire Moors Railway, owned by Sir Nigel Gresley Locomotive Preservation Trust Ltd and approved for mainline use, in BR blue livery.

UNION OF SOUTH AFRICA

NO 60009 (1937-66)

Based at Thornton Yard, Scotland, owned by John Cameron and approved for mainline use, in BR green livery. Originally built for the Coronation streamliner service.

DWIGHT D EISENHOWER

NO 60008 (1937-63)

Owned and based at National Railroad Museum, Green Bay, Wisconsin, USA, on static display, in BR green livery (currently in UK for Mallard 75 celebration in 2013). Originally built as No 4496 Golden Shuttle for the West Riding streamliner service.

A VISIT TO THE GREAT GATHERING
EVENT LEAVES DAILY MIRROR
JOURNALIST AND SELF-CONFESSED
TRAINSPOTTER PAUL ROUTLEDGE
FEELING SMITTEN, AS HE EXPLAINS
WHY MALLARD AND ITS SISTER
ENGINES WILL ALWAYS HAVE A
SPECIAL PLACE IN HIS HEART.

I f only they could speak, these beauties would sing Do Ya Think I'm Sexy? Mallard and her five sisters in sparkling garter blue or olive green, form a magical, glamorous line-up.

We're talking railway engines here, six members of Sir Nigel Gresley's A4 Pacific class, built in the 1930s to haul crack expresses on the LNER's London-Edinburgh route. They've been brought together at the National Railway Museum in York, to celebrate the 75th anniversary of 4468 Mallard breaking the world speed record for steam on Stoke Bank just south of Grantham, Lincolnshire.

Nothing like this has been seen since the demise of steam in 1968, and it's never likely to be repeated. 4489 Dominion of Canada was shipped over from a rail museum in Montreal.

60008 Dwight D Eisenhower, named after the US president and Second World War general, came across the pond from Green Bay, Wisconsin.

4464 Bittern got here under her own steam, touching 90mph on the journey from London. 60007 Sir Nigel Gresley is usually seen on the North Yorks Moors Railway. 60009 Union of South Africa is privately owned and works special trains. Mallard is on home ground, a static exhibit in the NRM.

Together, they make a formidable sight. Elegant, but charged with the enormous power of the most famous class of locomotives – "streaks" we called them as trainspotters – ever to run on British metals.

Paul Routledge on the footplate of Mallard, top, and the famous steam locomotive on display at the National Railway Museum

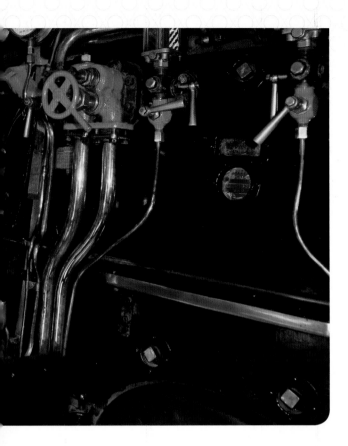

Now 8,000 people a day are flocking to the National Railway Museum to see "The Great Gathering" of these magnificent ladies (engines are always "she", perhaps because in those days the drivers were all men).

Frankly speaking, these girls and I have a long-standing love affair going back more than half a century to the days when they queened it on the East Coast Main Line hauling The Elizabethan, Flying Scotsman (a train as well as an engine), Yorkshire Pullman and suchlike famous expresses.

Tearing through Doncaster on the centre line, chime going full blast, they sent a shiver of delight through the crowd of small (and some not so small) boys on the platform.

Seated in luxury and served by waiters who would have looked at home in the Ritz, the passengers looked in some disdain at these noisy youngsters in short trousers and thick woollen socks down to their ankles, pencils and Ian Allen locospotters' books in hand.

We knew every "namer" – an engine

with a name, obviously – and their home shed. Mallard was shedded at King's Cross, coded 34A. Union of South Africa lived at 64B Edinburgh Haymarket.

We loved "streaks" the best. Their chime, a long, haunting note, was unique to the A4 Pacifics. It stayed in the mind's ear long after they had gone.

But here they are back in my life again. I'm in the driver's seat of Mallard, one hand on the regulator, eyes trained down the side of the boiler, looking for imaginary signals. And we can all relive the record ride on her bucking footplate in a scary simulator too.

So many people have family rail links. When they were nationalised in 1947, the railways employed hundreds of thousands of men and women in every form of activity from shunting to shaving in hotels, from porter to stationmaster.

My father was on the railway all his life, and I was born in a railway house. It's in the blood.

Today, the system is de-manned and privatised but the history and romance lives on at the museum, one of the North's most popular tourist venues.

Senior curator Anthony Coulls says: "This is one hell of a celebration, a once-in-a-lifetime opportunity to celebrate Mallard.

"There have been other anniversaries and there will be a 100th but this is the only chance we have to get all six engines together in one place." ■

"WE HAVE A LONG-STANDING LOVE AFFAIR GOING BACK MORE THAN HALF A CENTURY"

The Silver Jubilee crossing the
Welwyn Viaduct in the 1930s

MALLARD'S LEGACY

THE AGE OF STEAM MAY BE OVER BUT SIR NIGEL GRESLEY'S ACHIEVEMENTS LIVE ON AS BRITAIN, AGAINST ALL THE ODDS, SHOWS IT STILL HAS THE SPARK OF RAILWAY GENIUS

The London & North Eastern Railway developed a high-speed network, with the Silver Jubilee joined by the Coronation and West Riding streamlined trains in the late 1930s.

The fact we are still talking about them today shows how the determination of railway staff in every department made the services succeed and bring excitement back on track.

By the end of the decade, if the East Anglian London - Norwich service (with streamlined locos but ordinary coaches) is included, the LNER could boast four high-speed services totalling 1,952 miles a day, which added up to almost 10,000 miles weekly. ⊗

Below: **The Coronation train snaking its way out of Newcastle Central Station on July 2, 1937, en route to Edinburgh.**

⊙ There is a "train" of railway thought which argues that using steam power instead of diesel for streamlined services was a retrograde move. But is easy to forget how deeply bedded Britain was in coal-powered industry before the war.

Sir Nigel Gresley got it right with the A4s, as they were a logical progression with a technology familiar to railwaymen and used a locally-available fuel. No major re-engineering was needed for a new technology nor was there a need to import oil. Also, the locomotives were very versatile and could be used for other more mundane duties when not racing around with streamlined expresses.

The Second World War put a stop to the streamliners and any development of the concept which surely would have followed given their commercial success. As discussed, though, certain fundamental truths lurked in the background, awaiting their time again but with diesel and electric power. ⊙

"THE SECOND WORLD WAR PUT A STOP TO THE STREAMLINERS BUT CERTAIN FUNDAMENTAL TRUTHS LURKED IN THE BACKGROUND, AWAITING THEIR TIME AGAIN BUT WITH DIESEL AND ELECTRIC POWER"

Top: One of the powerful mainline diesel-electric locomotives built by British Railways under the modernisation programme is seen at Marylebone station, London, in April 1959. Named Scafell Pike, the locomotive was capable of hauling a heavy express passenger train at speeds of up to 90mph

Right: The new diesel-electric Midland Pullman train at St Pancras station in May 1960

The shape of travel to come

Takes off between Glasgow, Preston and London Euston

InterCity APT

The most Advanced Passenger Train

This is the age of the train ⇄

A BR Intercity 125 passing
through countryside in 1985

The Shinkansen bullet train speeding along a raised
railway line in the centre of Tokyo, Japan

⊙ Aerodynamic streamlining does allow trains to go faster at a cheaper cost. The public is in love with speed and the all-important image of high-speed travel is a vital marketing tool to increase use and revenue. By the 1960s the time was right for diesel and electric to take over the fastest trains.

This was typified by the Japanese Tokaido Shinkansen, the electric-powered "Bullet" trains which attracted worldwide fame from their introduction in 1964. Unfortunately, Britain's Advanced Passenger Train (APT), an experimental tilting high-speed electric train developed by British Rail during the 1970-early 1980s was cancelled by the government. This was after it set a new UK rail speed record of 152.3mph in 1975. Among the APT's pioneering technical advancements was the active tilting system, which has since been adopted on other high-speed designs around the world.

These include the Italian-built Pendolinos – the technology was sold to the Italians by British Rail – operated by Virgin Trains on the West Coast Main Line from 2003. In the meantime, the APT prototypes are preserved at NRM's Locomotion at Shildon.

What did succeed was the High Speed Train (HST), better known to the public as the InterCity 125, developed at the same time as the APT. BR managers wanted to hedge their bets on the next generation of trains. Just as Gresley and Stanier took steam to its limits, so BR engineers did with conventional diesel power.

Introduced in 1976, the InterCity 125 has gone on to become one of the most successful designs ever, moving millions of ordinary passengers on frequent interval services, not just an expense account business class on a once-a-day schedule. It was developed by Terry Miller, a Doncaster apprentice when Gresley was chief mechanical engineer. ⊙

> "AERODYNAMIC STREAMLINING DOES ALLOW TRAINS TO GO FASTER AT A CHEAPER COST"

⊘ These InterCity 125 express passenger multiple units are still in use more than three decades later and some are expected to last until 2035 on the ex-GWR London - Cornwall main line. This is an astonishing achievement showing that Britain, against all the odds, still has that spark of railway genius. Sir Nigel Gresley would be proud.

There are also plans, as part of the HS2 project, for a high-speed line to run between London and Birmingham from 2026, before being extended to Manchester and Leeds from 2033.

Our obsession with speed is definitely far from over. ■

Below: **A 140mph Hitachi 395 train at London's St Pancras International station in 2009**

The Birmingham and Fazeley viaduct, part of the proposed route for the HS2 high-speed rail scheme

KEEPING TRACK OF CLASSIC LOCOS

THE DISTINCTIVE SHAPE OF THE A4 LOCOS HAS ENSURED THEIR REGULAR APPEARANCES IN POPULAR CULTURE, FROM THEIR INTRODUCTION IN 1935 UP UNTIL THE PRESENT DAY.

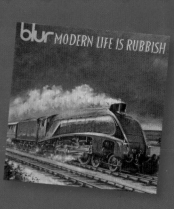

The first appearance of the A4s on film was by class leader No 2509 Silver Link in the celebrated comedy film Oh! Mr. Porter, of 1937, in which the star Will Hay soaks VIPs at the naming ceremony with a water crane.

No 60017 Silver Fox is the focus of the Elizabethan Express, of 1954, the British Transport Film showcasing the non-stop London - Edinburgh service. Five years later, the remade colour version of The Thirty-Nine Steps features No 60010 Dominion of Canada and other A4s in British Railways' green livery at Edinburgh Waverley Station and on the Forth Railway Bridge.

In the Rev W Awdry's The Railway Series books, No 4468 Mallard is mentioned in the book Gordon The High Speed

Engine, by Christopher Awdry. Mallard is in the later book Thomas And The Great Railway Show and in the TV version of the stories Thomas And Friends.

The cover of the 1993 Blur album Modern Life Is Rubbish is a painting of No 22 Mallard in garter blue by Paul Gribble, evoking a Boys' Own adventure story pre-war ambience.

British neo-prog band Big Big Train's song East Coast Racer, of 2013, recounts Mallard's record-breaking success. In the model world, mass production of A4s was begun by Hornby, of Liverpool in 1938. The later Hornby Dublo version was a big seller in the 1950-60s. Hornby, in its current manifestation, and rival Bachmann both produce ready-to-run 'OO' gauge A4s.

Message from the National Railway Museum: *Donations from many individual supporters of the National Railway Museum made the Mallard 75 celebrations possible. If you want to make a gift which will help us continue to celebrate our railway history please contact our Development team on: 01904 685774. In return, we'll take you closer to the history that you love through updates and invitations to special events.*

The museum is an exempt charity under the Second Schedule of the Charities Act (1960) and is recognised as charitable by Revenue & Customs. Our Revenue & Customs exemption number is XN63797A.